All Around Michigan

Regions and Resources

Alexandra Fix

Heinemann Library
Chicago, Illinois

© 2004 Heinemann Library
a division of Reed Elsevier Inc.
Chicago, Illinois

Customer Service 888-454-2279

Visit our website at www.heinemannlibrary.com

Designed by Heinemann Library
Photo research by Stephanie L. Miller
Printed in the United States by Lake Book
   Manufacturing, Inc.

08 07 06 05 04
10 9 8 7 6 5 4 3 2 1

**Library of Congress
Cataloging-in-Publication Data**
Fix, Alexandra, 1950-
  All around Michigan : regions and resources /
Alexandra Fix.
      v. cm. -- (Heinemann state studies)
  Includes bibliographical references (p.) and index.
  Contents: An introduction to Michigan -- Upper peninsula -- Northern lower peninsula -- Eastern lower peninsula -- Central lower peninsula -- Western lower peninsula.
   ISBN 1-4034-0658-8 -- ISBN 1-4034-2676-7 (pbk.)
   1. Michigan--Geography--Juvenile literature. 2. Regionalism--Michigan--Juvenile literature. [1. Michigan.] I. Title. II. Series.
   F566.3.F59 2003
   917.74--dc22
                                  2003017159

Acknowledgments
The author and publishers are grateful to the following for permission to reproduce copyright material:
Title page (L-R) Don Smetzer, Macduff Everton/Corbis, Robert Lifson/Heinemann Library; contents page, p. 18b John and Ann Mahan; p. 4 Ariel Skelley/Corbis; pp. 5, 7, 11, 13, 19, 27, 28, 35, 39, 45 Kimberly Saar/Heinemann Library; pp. 6, 8 maps.com/Heinemann Library; pp. 10, 20, 21, 24, 30, 37b, 42t Robert Lifson/Heinemann Library; pp. 12, 15t, 17, 22, 23, 37t Corbis; p. 13 Don Smetzer; p. 14 Phil Schermeister/Corbis; p. 15b D. Clark-O'Brien/Photri; p. 16t State Archives of Michigan; p. 16b Lowell Georgia/Corbis; p. 18t David Muench/Corbis; p. 25 Macduff Everton/Corbis; p. 26t Michigan DNR; p. 26b Courtesy of the Shrine of the Pines; p. 31 AFP/Corbis; p. 32 David Miller/Heinemann Library; p. 33t Carlos Osorio/AP Wide World Photos; p. 33b Horst Staudner/Omni-Photo Communications; p. 34 Joseph Sohm/ChromoSohm Inc./Corbis; p. 35 Courtesy of Michigan State University; p. 38 Michigan Space Center; p. 40t Grace Davies/Omni-Photo Communications; p. 40b The Advertising Archive; p. 41 Dennis Cox; p. 42b Richard Hamilton Smith/Corbis; p. 43 Brian Forde/Holland Sentinel/AP Wide World Photos; p. 44t Nichole Thieda/Heinemann Library; p. 44b Progressive AE and Ellerbe Becket - Architects and Engineers of DeVos Place

Cover photographs by (top, L-R) Ariel Skelley/Corbis, Joseph Sohm/ChromoSohm Inc./Corbis, Robert Lifson/Heinemann Library, Robert Lifson/Heinemann Library; (main) James L. Amos/Corbis

The publisher would like to thank Charlene Rimsa for her assistance with this book.

Special thanks to Bernice Anne Houseward for her curriculum guidance.

Every effort has been made to contact copyright holders of any material reproduced in this book. Any omissions will be rectified in subsequent printings if notice is given to the publisher.

Some words are shown in bold, **like this.** You can find out what they mean by looking in the glossary.

Contents

An Introduction to Michigan

Michigan is often called a "Water Wonderland." No matter where people stand in Michigan, they are never more than 6 miles from a lake, river, or stream. The most a person would have to travel to reach one of the Great Lakes is only 85 miles. For work and play, people in Michigan use their land, lakes, and rivers everyday.

LOCATION

Michigan is part of a large group of states called the Midwest and part of a smaller group within the Midwest, called the Great Lakes states. Michigan is made up of two separate **peninsulas** with no land connection to each other. The Upper Peninsula of Michigan connects to Wisconsin. Lake Superior, Lake Michigan, and Lake Huron surround this land mass. This whole portion of the state is commonly called the Upper Peninsula or the U.P. The southern border of the Lower Peninsula of Michigan is Indiana and Ohio. This land area is surrounded by Lakes Michigan, Huron, and Erie. Michigan is divided into 83 counties, with 15 in the Upper Peninsula and 68 in the Lower Peninsula.

Boating is a popular pastime in Michigan. There are close to one million registered boats in the state!

Michigan's Regions

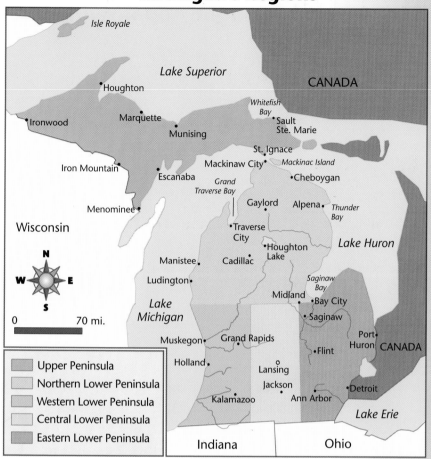

Michigan covers 56,804 square miles. In size, Michigan ranks 22nd in the United States. Michigan has 9.9 million residents. In population, it ranks 8th in the United States.

REGIONS OF MICHIGAN

Michigan can be divided into three main regions: the Upper Peninsula, the northern Lower Peninsula, and the southern Lower Peninsula. The southern Lower Peninsula can be further divided into the eastern Lower Peninsula, central Lower Peninsula, and western Lower Peninsula. Looking at the Lower Peninsula as a mitten shape, the northern Lower Peninsula would be the fingers and the southern Lower Peninsula would be the palm and thumb. In Michigan, 86 percent of the state's residents live in the southern Lower Peninsula, 11 percent live in the northern Lower Peninsula, and 3 percent live in the entire Upper Peninsula.

MICHIGAN'S LAND AND WATER

The Lower Peninsula and the eastern half of the Upper Peninsula are part of a land region called the Great Lakes Plains. The surface ranges from flat land to gently rolling hills. There are sections of swamp or **wetland.**

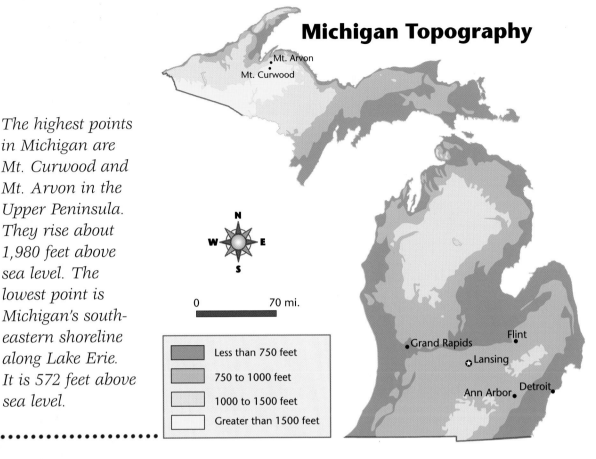

Michigan Topography

- Mt. Arvon
- Mt. Curwood

N
W E
S

0 ——————— 70 mi.

■	Less than 750 feet
■	750 to 1000 feet
□	1000 to 1500 feet
□	Greater than 1500 feet

- Grand Rapids
- Flint
- Lansing
- Ann Arbor
- Detroit

The highest points in Michigan are Mt. Curwood and Mt. Arvon in the Upper Peninsula. They rise about 1,980 feet above sea level. The lowest point is Michigan's south-eastern shoreline along Lake Erie. It is 572 feet above sea level.

Forests cover half of the state. There are high sand dunes in the western side of the Lower Peninsula, all along the Lake Michigan shoreline. There are also **inland** sand dunes in some areas of the Upper Peninsula and near Lake Huron.

The western half of the Upper Peninsula is called the Superior Upland. It is rocky with forested hillsides that range from 600 to 1,980 feet above sea level. The highest areas are located along the Lake Superior shore.

Water plays an important part in this "Water Wonderland" state. Lake Ontario is the only one of the five Great Lakes that does not touch Michigan's border. The Great Lakes cover more than 94,000 square miles and contain 1/5 of the world's fresh surface water, about 6 quadrillion gallons. Michigan also has 3,288 miles of shoreline. All of Michigan's shoreline added together equals more than the distance along the Atlantic Ocean from Maine to Florida.

Besides the Great Lakes, Michigan also has more than 11,000 inland lakes and more than 36,000 miles of rivers and streams. There are also more than 150 waterfalls in Michigan.

MICHIGAN'S CLIMATE

Michigan has a **semi-maritime climate** because of the Great Lakes surrounding it. The state experiences four distinct seasons. There is often a difference of about 10° F between the northern and southern parts of the state. The Upper Peninsula is usually cooler than the Lower Peninsula. Because of this, the Upper Peninsula usually receives far more snow than an area such as Detroit on the southeastern side of the state. The growing season is shortest in the interior of the Upper Peninsula and longest near Lake Michigan in the southwestern Lower Peninsula.

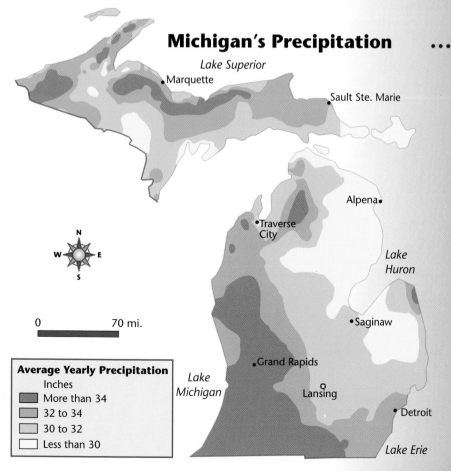

Michigan's Precipitation

Lake Superior
•Marquette
Sault Ste. Marie
Alpena•
•Traverse City
Lake Huron
•Saginaw
•Grand Rapids
Lake Michigan
Lansing
•Detroit
Lake Erie

0   70 mi.

Average Yearly Precipitation
Inches
More than 34
32 to 34
30 to 32
Less than 30

Most rain in Michigan falls during the summer. The heaviest snowfalls are usually in December and January. Michigan also has many cloudy days. In summer, 6 of every 10 days are partly cloudy. In winter, 7 of every 10 days are partly cloudy.

Michigan's Resources

Regions
- Upper Peninsula
- Northern Lower Peninsula
- Eastern Lower Peninsula
- Central Lower Peninsula
- Western Lower Peninsula

Agriculture
- Grapes
- Beans
- Wheat
- Rye
- Hogs
- Corn
- Berries
- Potatoes
- Hay
- Fruit
- Sheep
- Poultry
- Oats
- Soybeans
- Vegetables
- Sugar beets
- Cattle
- Dairy products

Mining
- Sand, gravel
- Copper
- Iron Ore
- Gypsum
- Stone

Natural Resources
- Oil
- Natural gas
- Salt

Industry
- Nursery products
- Manufacturing

Michigan's ranks first in the country in production of tart cherries, dry beans, blueberries, pickling cucumbers, red "new" potatoes, potatoes for chips, geraniums, hanging flower baskets, and Easter lilies.

MICHIGAN'S RESOURCES

Michigan's valuable **natural resources** include water, land, forests, minerals, **fertile** soil, plants, and animals. Each adds to the beauty of the state for residents and tourists. Work and play are shaped by the resources found in a region. Iron and copper in the Upper Peninsula led to mining. Large forests in the northern Lower Peninsula led to logging. Fertile soil created rich farmlands in the southern Lower Peninsula. Some of Michigan's natural resources, especially wood and iron **ore,** have been used in the automobile and furniture **industries.** Michigan's water has provided good transportation to ship all of the Michigan products to distant states. The ways in which people have used Michigan's resources have affected the settlement, growth, and development of the state.

Manufacturing Industry

This state leads the United States in automobile **manufacturing.** Michigan also produces other transportation-related items, machinery, office furniture, appliances, baby food, chemicals, **pharmaceuticals,** and lumber.

Tourism Industry

Each year, about 25 million people visit Michigan. **Tourism** is the second most important industry in the state. Tourists spend about $10 billion in the state each year. One of the big draws to Michigan is its land. Michigan has 96 state parks, 6 state forests, 4 national parks, and 3 national forests.

The Michigan Economy
Its Natural, Capital, and Human Resources
Gross State Product (in dollars)

Manufacturing	$85.5 billion
Services	$64.9 billion
Retail & Wholesale	$53.6 billion
Finance, Insurance & Real Estate	$46.4 billion
Government	$33.3 billion
Transportation & Utilities	$21.3 billion
Construction	$16.6 billion
Agriculture	$2.9 billion
Mining	less than $0.5 million

Total Gross State Product: $325.4 billion

*Michigan's $325.4 billion gross state product makes it the 9th largest state **economy** in the United States.*

Farming is a family tradition in Michigan. There are about 6,000 Michigan farms bigger than 10 acres that have been owned by the same family for over 100 years.

AGRICULTURE INDUSTRY

Agriculture is the third most important **industry** in Michigan. There are 52,000 farms in Michigan covering a total of 10.4 million acres. Eighty percent of Michigan's farms are located across the southern part of Michigan, from east to west.

MICHIGAN'S TRANSPORTATION

The lakes and rivers of Michigan have always been its first natural transportation routes. The 50 **port** cities on the Great Lakes, the Soo Locks, the Erie Canal, and the St. Lawrence Seaway connected Michigan's waterways to distant states and to the Atlantic Ocean. Today, almost 30 million tons of **cargo** are shipped each year from Detroit's ports alone.

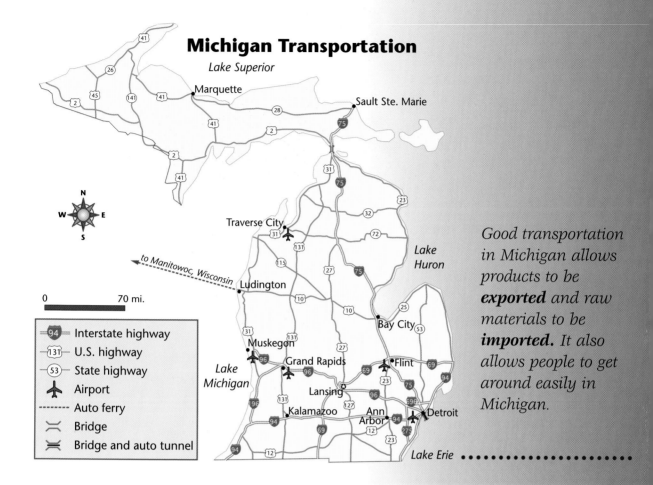

Michigan Transportation

Lake Superior

Marquette

Sault Ste. Marie

to Manitowoc, Wisconsin

Ludington

Lake Huron

Traverse City

Bay City

Muskegon

Grand Rapids

Flint

Lake Michigan

Lansing

Kalamazoo

Ann Arbor

Detroit

Lake Erie

0   70 mi.

- 94 Interstate highway
- 131 U.S. highway
- 53 State highway
- ✈ Airport
- ----- Auto ferry
- ✕ Bridge
- ✕ Bridge and auto tunnel

*Good transportation in Michigan allows products to be **exported** and raw materials to be **imported.** It also allows people to get around easily in Michigan.*

The first real roads followed the trails made by Native Americans. While Michigan was still a **territory,** the first highway, the Chicago Road, crossed the southern Lower Peninsula from Lake Erie to Lake Michigan. When lumber was plentiful, roads were often paved with hardwood logs or wooden planks. In the 1900s, state highways were built, and in the 1950s, interstate expressways were constructed. Today, Michigan has about 120,000 miles of roads. There are also five railroad lines that carry cargo around the state and one rail line that carries passengers across the southern Lower Peninsula to Chicago.

Upper Peninsula

The Upper Peninsula became part of Michigan after settling a fight with Ohio. When Ohio became a state in 1803, they claimed a section of land called the Toledo Strip. This was important property because it included a **port** on Lake Erie. The people in the Michigan **Territory** insisted that the Toledo Strip belonged to them. Before Michigan could become a state, this border dispute needed to be settled. In 1836, President Andrew Jackson gave the Toledo Strip to Ohio and 9,000 acres in the western Upper Peninsula to Michigan. Although the people of Michigan were upset at first, the Upper Peninsula turned out to be a valuable piece of property, rich in copper and iron **ore,** and very important to Michigan.

For years, the only way visitors could reach the Upper Peninsula was to take a car ferry across the water or drive all the way around Lake Michigan, through Illinois and Wisconsin, and into the Upper Peninsula. During deer hunting season, people would often wait for almost six hours to cross in a ferry. Cars were backed up for miles. It was not until 1957 that the five-mile long

During Labor Day morning each year, two lanes of the Mackinac Bridge are closed to cars so people can walk across the bridge.

The Upper Peninsula is 384 miles long and 233 miles wide. It is bigger than the four states of Connecticut, Delaware, Massachusetts, and Rhode Island put together.

Mackinac (pronounced MACK-in-aw) Bridge was completed. The bridge took three years to build and is one of the world's longest suspension bridges.

LOCATION AND MAJOR CITIES

Much of the Upper Peninsula is **sparsely** settled. The region contains 25 percent of the land belonging to Michigan, but only 3 percent of the population. Only three Upper Peninsula cities have a population greater than 13,000 people.

The largest city in the Upper Peninsula is Marquette, which began as a mining town. Today it is the center of government and **commerce** in the region.

Houghton is home to Michigan Technological University. This is one of the top 50 universities in the United States. However, its students really have to love cold weather, because winter lasts for most of the school year. In the winter of 1949–1950, Houghton had 276.5 inches of snow.

Sault Ste. Marie is the oldest continually settled area in the Midwest. It began as a trading post in 1650. The Soo Locks are located in this city.

Michigan's Upper Peninsula

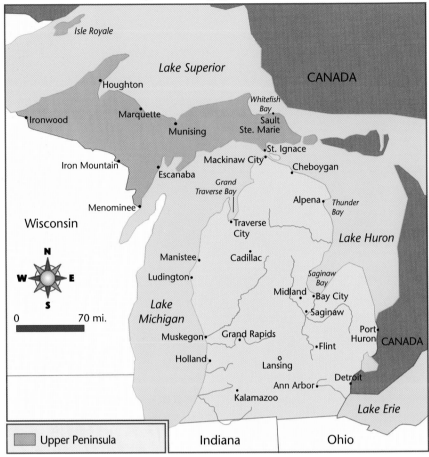

Isle Royale

Lake Superior

CANADA

Houghton

Whitefish Bay

Ironwood

Marquette

Sault Ste. Marie

Munising

St. Ignace

Iron Mountain

Mackinaw City

Cheboygan

Escanaba

Grand Traverse Bay

Alpena

Thunder Bay

Menominee

Wisconsin

Traverse City

Lake Huron

Manistee

Cadillac

Ludington

Saginaw Bay

Midland

Bay City

Saginaw

Lake Michigan

Port Huron

CANADA

Muskegon

Grand Rapids

Flint

Holland

Lansing

Detroit

Ann Arbor

Kalamazoo

Lake Erie

N W E S

0   70 mi.

Upper Peninsula | Indiana | Ohio

LAND AND WATER

The eastern portion of the Upper Peninsula is generally flat and often swampy. In the western portion of the Upper Peninsula, the land becomes hilly and tree-covered. There are small mountain ranges, including the Gogebic, Menominee, and Marquette Ranges and the Huron and Porcupine Mountains. Elevations in the western Upper Peninsula range from 600 to 1,980 feet.

Soo Locks at Sault Ste. Marie

Because of the locks, large ships are able to sail between Lake Superior and Lake Huron and bypass the rapids of the St. Mary's River. The locks lower or raise ships in the canal in order to make up for a 21-foot difference in the water levels of the two lakes.

CLIMATE

The Upper Peninsula is the coldest region of Michigan. Even in the summer when the days are warm, the nights can be cold. In Houghton, the average low temperature in January is 7°F and the average high in July is 74°F. The lowest recorded temperature in Marquette was −34°F in 1979. The average annual rainfall is 37.1 inches. The average annual snowfall is 177.6 inches.

The highest official Michigan snowfall was 391.9 inches at Delaware, Michigan, on the Keweenaw Peninsula, during the winter of 1978–1979. However, it is not uncommon to have close to this much **lake effect** snow in this region each year. This is great for the skiing and snowmobiling **industries.**

The white-tailed deer is a Michigan state symbol. There are about two million deer here, more than any other state except Texas.

COPPER MINING INDUSTRY

Thousands of years ago, the Old Copper Indians discovered copper in the rocky ground of the Keweenaw Peninsula. They used this mineral to make their weapons and tools. In 1840, state **geologist** Douglass Houghton rediscovered the presence of copper there. Suddenly, miners came to Michigan for adventure. Three years before the Gold Rush in California, the Copper Rush in Michigan reached its peak. From 1846 until 1887, Michigan led in the production of copper. No Michigan copper mines are in operation today.

Shaft-rockhouses, like the one pictured here, would separate the rock from the copper that was mined from the ground.

IRON ORE MINING INDUSTRY

In 1844, iron was discovered in the Marquette Range. It was later found in the Menominee and Gogebic Ranges also. Many **immigrants** came with their families to the Upper Peninsula to work in the mines. Communities began to grow, and the iron **industry** has been strong for 125 years. Michigan's two remaining mines still produce nearly one-quarter of the iron **ore** mined in the U.S. today.

Both the construction of the Erie Canal in 1825 and the opening of the Soo Locks in 1855 were of major importance to Michigan. They allowed the Upper Peninsula to ship copper and iron by water to distant places. It also made it easier for people to come to Michigan to work and live. Settlers could now make part of their trip to Michigan by water. This saved the pioneers many miles of difficult travel on land.

AGRICULTURE INDUSTRY

The growing season in the Upper Peninsula is short. In some places it lasts only 60 days. The major farm product in the region is **livestock,** especially cattle and dairy products. Potatoes are also an important **cash crop** in some areas.

*The countries Michigan **exports** the most products to are Canada, Mexico, and Japan.*

LOGGING AND SAWMILL INDUSTRY

Escanaba and Menominee became centers for the lumber industry. Logs were moved down the long Escanaba and Menominee Rivers, sawed into lumber, and transported by boat down Lake Michigan to Chicago. Logging continues to be important today. Almost 85 percent of the Upper Peninsula is forest. Today, logs are used to supply **pulp** to papermills in Escanaba, Munising, and Iron Mountain.

TOURISM

Tourism has become an important industry. People come to the Upper Peninsula to enjoy skiing, camping, hiking, kayaking, hunting, and fishing. Much of the region is wild and undisturbed. A few highways crisscross the **peninsula** to connect the cities that are many miles apart.

When loggers cut down trees today, they plant new trees to replace the ones they took out of the forest.

TOURIST ATTRACTIONS AND PLACES OF INTEREST

A ship bell from the sunken *Edmund Fitzgerald* tolls at the Great Lakes Shipwreck Museum at Whitefish Point. This part of Lake Superior is called the "Graveyard of the Great Lakes." Rocky shorelines and violent storms can be deadly for ships. In 1913 alone, 40 ships sank here. From Munising, tourists can ride in a glass bottom boat to see the remains of several sunken shipwrecks.

A U.P. Food Favorite

A favorite food of the U.P. is the pasty (pronounced PAST-ee). The miners from Cornwall, England, brought this recipe to Michigan from their homeland. Roast beef, potatoes, onions, rutabagas, and carrots are wrapped in a pastry crust. The men would bring these small pies to the mines in tin pails. At mealtime, they would put the pail over a candle and heat their pasty.

Over 50,000 gallons of water tumble over Tahquamenon Falls every second!

Tahquamenon Falls is Michigan's most famous waterfall. It is located in the eastern Upper Peninsula, south of Whitefish Point. Its brown water is caused by **tannin** deposits and the white foam is created by the force of the waterfall. It looks like root beer.

A boat ride is the best way to see Pictured Rocks National Lakeshore. Waves, winds, and rain have carved these colored sandstone cliffs on Lake Superior.

The northernmost point of Michigan is an island. Isle Royale is one of the least visited national parks in the U.S. It is a **remote** wilderness with timber wolves, moose, fox, and other wildlife. It is a 4 1/2 hour boat ride from the Keweenaw Peninsula to reach Isle Royale.

Animals such as this red fox make their homes on Isle Royale. Isle Royale is 99 percent wilderness.

Northern Lower Peninsula

There is no distinct dividing line where southern Michigan ends and northern Michigan begins, but if you travel toward the top of the state, you notice the difference. The air becomes cooler, the woods thicker, the hills higher, and the cities and towns smaller and further apart. Only 11 percent of Michigan's residents live in this region.

Michigan's Northern Lower Peninsula

Lake Superior

CANADA

Houghton

Ironwood

Marquette

Sault Ste. Marie

Iron Mountain

Mackinaw City

Mackinac Island

Cheboygan

Grand Traverse Bay

Wisconsin

Gaylord

Alpena

Thunder Bay

Traverse City

Houghton Lake

Lake Huron

Manistee

Cadillac

Ludington

Saginaw Bay

Midland

Bay City

Saginaw

Muskegon

Grand Rapids

Port Huron

CANADA

Holland

Flint

Lansing

Detroit

Lake Michigan

Ann Arbor

Kalamazoo

Lake Erie

Northern Lower Peninsula

Indiana

Ohio

N W E S

0   70 mi.

LOCATION AND MAJOR CITIES

Many of the larger cities in the northern Lower Peninsula are scattered along the shores of the Great Lakes. A few larger cities are located where there are clusters of **inland** lakes and rivers.

Traverse City is the largest city in the northern Lower Peninsula. Located on Lake Michigan's Grand Traverse Bay, this is a popular **resort** town. Gaylord, in the center of this region, enjoys the claim of being exactly halfway between the equator and the North Pole. Alpena is an old lumber town, located on the Lake Huron side of this region. Mackinaw City was once a French trading post. The Mackinac Bridge begins in this city and crosses over the Straits of Mackinac to St. Ignace in the Upper Peninsula.

Huge dunes at Sleeping Bear Dunes National Lakeshore rise to 465 feet.

LAND AND WATER

The lower part of the northern Lower Peninsula is flat land with some rolling hills. Higher elevations are in the northern center of this region. Gaylord is the highest point in the Lower Peninsula at 1,348 feet above sea level. White pine and mixed hardwood trees cover the region. The northern Lower Peninsula is famous for its trout streams. The Pere Marquette, AuSable, and Manistee Rivers are the most well known. The largest inland lake in Michigan is Houghton Lake, which is also located here. It covers 31.8 square miles. In addition, there are areas of rocky soil, sand, and swamp. Sand dunes line the shores of Lake Michigan.

Almost four out of every ten trees in the state of Michigan are in the Lower Peninsula.

CLIMATE

Because of the higher elevation and more northern location, this region tends to have colder winters and a much shorter growing season than southern parts of the state. Gaylord gets an average of 150 inches of snow each year. The average annual rainfall is 35.7 inches. The average high temperature in July is 81°F and the average low temperature in January is 9°F.

LOGGING AND SAWMILL INDUSTRIES

Water and woods have played an important part in northern Michigan's **economy.** As pioneers moved westward in the United States, lumber was needed to build homes and businesses. The forests of Maine and New York had been logged heavily and Michigan was the next good source for lumber. Michigan's white pines grow tall, straight, and strong, and make excellent lumber. By the 1800s, some of these trees were 200 feet tall and 5 feet around. A single tree could provide enough wood to build a 5-room house.

In 1840, loggers began to clear the forests of northern Michigan. Logs were cut into lumber at the sawmills, which were built beside the rivers. Water power from the rivers ran the sawmill machinery. By the time the Civil War (1861–1865) ended, lumber had become a major Michigan **industry.** At first, the rivers were the main method to transport logs to the sawmills. Lumberjacks cut down trees year-round, but needed the cover of snow to transport the heavy logs. Horses would pull huge piles of logs by sled over the icy roads to the riverbanks. When the spring thaw came, logs were carried down the river on the strong currents to the sawmills.

In the 1870s, two **innovations** helped loggers to depend less on the weather to get the logs to the sawmills. One great idea was called the Big Wheels. Logs were attached to an **axle** between two large wheels and pulled by a team of horses. Another invention was the narrow gauge railroad, used for transporting logs from distant woods.

Once there were easier ways to move logs, hardwood trees could be harvested. Pine had floated, but hardwood was too heavy. Now hardwoods could also be cut for lumber. From 1869 to 1899, Michigan was the leading United States producer of lumber.

River drivers had the dangerous job of riding the logs down the river and breaking up log jams.

Big wheels were invented by Silas C. Overpack. Overpack's wheels were always painted red.

Unfortunately, early logging companies had not considered the future of the forests and had not replanted trees. The supply of lumber ran out. Michigan learned a hard lesson from that mistake. In the 1930s, during the Great Depression, a **reforestation** project took place. People who were looking for jobs joined the Civilian Conservation Corps and planted 484 million trees. Today, loggers practice **conservation.** Michigan plants twice as many trees as it harvests.

Today, logging continues to be important to Michigan's **economy.** There are still 276 sawmills, 14 veneer mills, 8 **pulp** and paper mills, and 18 wood-using plants in the state.

AGRICULTURE INDUSTRY

When the forests were cleared, some settlers tried to farm the land. The soil and **climate** were not good enough to grow strong crops. Many of these farms failed and much of the land returned to ownership by the state. Today, this state land is an important part of the tourist **industry,** used for camping, hunting, and fishing.

The average tart cherry tree has 7,000 cherries.

One thing did grow well in the cleared forests. Cherry trees sprang up where other trees had been cut down. By the time logging was finished in the area, cherry trees had begun to **thrive** and bear fruit. Today, Traverse City is the "Cherry Capital of the World." The area grows 75 percent of all tart cherries in the U.S. and 20 percent of all sweet cherries.

MINERALS

Stores of oil and natural gas have been found in the ground in the area around the Pigeon River, in the northern center of this region. These products are **extracted** and used around the state as fuel for heating and cooking.

TOURISM

Today, one of the most important **industries** in the northern Lower Peninsula is **tourism.** Many people head north each season to enjoy nature. Summer is great for camping, fishing, boating, swimming, and golfing. The beaches of the Great Lakes and the **inland** lakes are always popular. In the fall, sunny days and frosty nights turn the green leaves to red and gold. Many people take tours to see the changing leaves, driving through the northern woods. Hunting is also popular in this region. Michigan is second in the United States in deer population. In the winter, visitors enjoy snowmobiling, skiing, sledding, skating, snow boarding, and ice fishing. Spring is a perfect time for riding bicycles, learning to golf, or fishing for trout and pike in the rivers and streams.

Tourist Attractions and Places of Interest

Mackinac Island is three miles long and three miles wide. People can reach the island by boat or plane. This is a fun place to imagine the "olden days," because no motorized vehicles such as cars or motorcycles are allowed on the island. Residents and tourists walk or ride bicycles or horse-drawn carriages around the island.

At Hartwick Pines State Park, in Grayling, visitors can glimpse the beauty of northern Michigan's forests of the past. The forest is 49 acres of uncut, original pine forest. The trees are so tall that the branches begin more than 80 feet above the ground.

Between 500 and 600 people live on Mackinac Island year-round. Tourists to the area are called "fudgies" because nearly everyone buys some of the famous island fudge to take home.

Hartwick Pines State Park is named after Edward E. Hartwick, a lumberman who was killed during World War I.

In Baldwin there is a log cabin called Shrine of the Pines. All of the furniture in the cabin is hand-carved from tree stumps and roots left behind when the white pine forests were logged.

Fort Mackinac and Fort Michilimackinac both played important parts in the American Revolution (1775–1783). There are tours and **authentic reenactments** at both **forts.**

A man named Raymond Overholzer crafted the furniture in the Shrine of the Pines without using metal fasteners of any kind.

Eastern Lower Peninsula

When people in Michigan talk about the east side of the state, they usually mean Detroit and its surrounding area. The eastern Lower Peninsula is known throughout the world for the production of automobiles. Detroit is often referred to as the "Motor City." This region has also been important for logging, shipbuilding, shipping, and **agriculture.**

Michigan's Eastern Lower Peninsula

- Lake Superior
- CANADA
- Houghton
- Ironwood
- Marquette
- Sault Ste. Marie
- St. Ignace
- Iron Mountain
- Mackinaw City
- Cheboygan
- Grand Traverse Bay
- Alpena
- Thunder Bay
- Wisconsin
- Traverse City
- Lake Huron
- Manistee
- Cadillac
- Ludington
- Saginaw Bay
- Midland
- Bay City
- Saginaw
- N W E S
- 0   70 mi.
- Port Huron
- CANADA
- Muskegon
- Grand Rapids
- Flint
- Holland
- Lansing
- Detroit
- Lake Michigan
- Ann Arbor
- Kalamazoo
- Lake Erie
- Eastern Lower Peninsula
- Indiana
- Ohio

LOCATION AND MAJOR CITIES

The eastern Lower Peninsula is the land along the Saginaw Bay, Lake Huron, Lake St. Clair, and Lake Erie. Included in this region is a part of Michigan commonly called the Thumb because of its location on the state's "mitten" shape.

Detroit is the oldest city in the Lower Peninsula. It was established in 1701 and many early settlers came to Michigan through Detroit. Detroit is now the largest city in Michigan and the tenth largest city in the United States. According to the 2000 U.S. Census, there are 951,270 people living in the city of Detroit. **Metropolitan** Detroit includes almost 100 cities surrounding Detroit and has a total population of about 4.4 million people. Metropolitan Detroit covers only 1/30 of the area of Michigan, but contains half the population of the entire state.

*In the Upper Peninsula, there is an average of 20 persons per square mile. The Lower Peninsula is more **densely** settled with an average of 230 persons per square mile. Metropolitan Detroit has an average of 1,140 persons per square mile.*

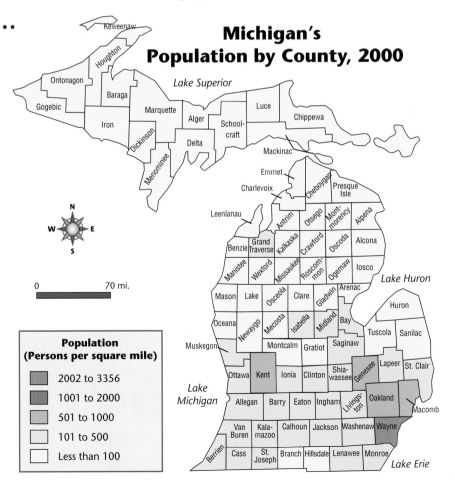

Michigan's Population by County, 2000

Population (Persons per square mile)

- 2002 to 3356
- 1001 to 2000
- 501 to 1000
- 101 to 500
- Less than 100

Fire Dangers

Huron City is a quiet little town on the northern part of the Thumb. It was once very busy with logging. After loggers had cut down all the trees in an area, the stumps and treetops were just left on the ground. These became very dry and easily caught fire. The Great Thumb Fire of 1881 destroyed the remaining trees in the area and the town never grew large again. Forest fire was a common danger with **overcutting.**

Ann Arbor is home to the University of Michigan. Founded in 1817, this is the oldest state university in the United States. In 1837, the school moved from Detroit to Ann Arbor, onto 40 acres of land. The Ann Arbor campus has grown big enough to cover 3,075 acres of land.

Saginaw and Bay City became important in the lumbering **era** of the 1800s. Many sawmills were built near the rivers to cut the logs from the region, and busy towns grew up around the sawmills. Because of the Saginaw River's location near the Great Lakes, many of those logs were used in shipbuilding.

Port Huron was once a lumber town also. The St. Clair River here links Lake Huron and Lake Erie. This city has also been involved in shipbuilding, railroading, and oil and natural gas distribution.

LAND AND WATER

The eastern Lower Peninsula land is mostly flat. The lowest point in Michigan is on the shoreline of Lake Erie at 572 feet above sea level. The Lake Huron and Lake Erie shorelines do not have the high sand dunes found on the western side of the state along Lake Michigan.

CLIMATE

It tends to be warmer on this side of the state than anywhere else in Michigan. The average low temperature in January is 16°F. The average high temperature in July is 83°F. Rainfall averages 33 inches per year and snowfall averages 43 inches per year. The **lake effect** factor does not affect this region, because the westerly winds move across the Great Lakes instead of toward land.

AUTOMOBILE INDUSTRY

The eastern Lower Peninsula has been in the business of building vehicles for a long time. In the 1870s, when the logging **industry** was booming in the state, Silas Overpack of Flint built the Big Wheels that were used to transport logs to the sawmills. Later, businesses in Flint continued to build wagons, carts, and horse-drawn carriages, and Flint became known as the "Vehicle City." General Motors would begin there and many automobile parts factories are located in Flint today.

As settlers moved west, there was a growing need for lumber all over the country. Ships and railroads were needed to transport lumber. Before it became a leader in the automobile industry, Detroit was an important center for the building of ships, railroad cars, tracks, and bridges.

The automobile industry came next. Around 1896, both Henry Ford and Ransom Olds were working on building

Ford Motor Company's most popular car ever was the Model T. It cost $850 when it was introduced in 1908. Ford's idea of the assembly line cut costs so much that by 1924, the same car cost only $290.

The headquarters for the three major United States automobile companies are in metropolitan Detroit. Ford Motor Company is in Dearborn. DaimlerChrysler has its American headquarters in Auburn Hills. General Motors Corporation, seen here, is in downtown Detroit.

a gas-powered engine for an automobile. Ford's success led to the Ford Motor Company in Detroit and Olds' success led to the Oldsmobile Company in Lansing.

When the United States entered World War II in 1941, the factories in the Detroit area switched from producing cars to making war products such as tanks, guns, aircraft, **ammunition,** and other parts. Michigan became known as the "**Arsenal** of Democracy." They produced 20 percent of America's defense war goods. After World War II ended in 1945, Detroit went back to making cars. The returning soldiers were eager to buy cars.

Today, the Detroit area, Flint, and Lansing produce more cars, buses, and trucks than any other part of the United States. Vehicle **manufacturing** is Michigan's number one industry. Michigan's top industry actually helped build Michigan's second-most important industry, which is tourism. Once people owned cars, they could travel.

MINING INDUSTRY

The Saginaw area has been a source for gypsum, which is used in construction material. Salt is found in abundance in the region of the St. Clair and Detroit Rivers. It has been **extracted** for many years, but there is still 70 trillion tons of salt under the city of Detroit.

AGRICULTURE INDUSTRY

The best farmland in the eastern Lower Peninsula is in three different areas: near Saginaw, across the northern area of the Thumb, and in the southeast corner of the state, below metropolitan Detroit.

When the trees from the Thumb area were all cut or burned down, the land was left flat and **barren.** In the 1890s, the professors at Michigan **Agricultural** College, now Michigan State University, in East Lansing came up with a plan to use the land in a different way. They determined that the **climate** and soil were well-suited to growing sugar beets and dry beans. These crops are still the most important **industry** in the Thumb and Saginaw Valley. The eastern Lower Peninsula is first in the United States in the production of dry beans and fourth in the production of sugar beets, which are used to make sugar.

Approximately 30,000 cars participate in the Woodward Dream Cruise events each year.

The southern part of the eastern Lower Peninsula has a long growing season and good soil. Milk, poultry, vegetables, and fruits are produced. **Metropolitan** Detroit is also known as one of the leading producers of greenhouse plants in the nation.

TOURIST ATTRACTIONS AND PLACES OF INTEREST

Every August, the Detroit area sponsors the Woodward Dream Cruise. In this event, 30,000 **vintage** vehicles drive down Woodward Avenue through some of the **suburbs** of Detroit. This street is perfect for the event as a part of Woodward Avenue was the first concrete pavement in

Detroit is home to several professional sports teams. The Red Wings hockey, Tigers baseball, Pistons and Shock basketball, and Lions football teams are all located here.

the United States as well as a test track for Henry Ford's cars.

Henry Ford bought many famous houses and **artifacts** and moved them to Greenfield Village and Henry Ford Museum in Dearborn. He bought the actual bike shop in which the Wright Brothers built the first airplane. He moved the workshop where Thomas Edison developed the light bulb all the way from New Jersey to his village. In the museum is the chair in which President Lincoln was **assassinated** and the bus in which Rosa Parks made her **civil rights** stand. The history of the automobile is told with hundreds of cars from the past.

Ann Arbor has some great dinosaur skeletons, a **mastodon** skeleton, and interesting exhibits at the University of Michigan Exhibit Museum of Natural History.

Frankenmuth is sometimes called "Michigan's Little Bavaria." It looks like a small European village with shops and parks. Bronner's, in Frankenmuth, is the largest year-round Christmas store in the world. It is the size of five-and-a-half football fields.

Girls in traditional German costumes dance at Frankenmuth's yearly Bavarian Festival.

Central Lower Peninsula

Lansing, the **capital** of Michigan, is located in the central Lower Peninsula, but this region is more than just a center for government. The central Lower Peninsula is an interesting blend of government offices, **industries,** and farmland.

*Michigan's **Capitol** building is modeled after the U.S. Capitol in Washington, D.C.*

LOCATION AND MAJOR CITIES

Lansing was not always the capital of Michigan. When Michigan was still a **territory,** the capital was located in Detroit. As the state grew, there were two important reasons to move the capital from Detroit. Detroit is on the eastern side of the state and shares a border with Canada. Many **citizens** were worried about the dangers of having the governing city so close to another country. They thought that enemies could endanger the city, and somewhere **inland** would be safer. Also, Michiganians wanted a city more central to the state, so Lansing was chosen in 1847. At that time, Lansing only had a small group of cabins near a sawmill on the Grand River. Lansing grew quickly and is now the sixth largest city in the state with a population of approximately 119,000 people.

Michigan's Central Lower Peninsula

- Houghton
- Ironwood
- Marquette
- Sault Ste. Marie
- Iron Mountain
- St. Ignace
- Mackinaw City
- Cheboygan
- Grand Traverse Bay
- Alpena
- Thunder Bay
- Wisconsin
- Traverse City
- Lake Huron
- Manistee
- Cadillac
- Ludington
- Saginaw Bay
- Midland
- Bay City
- Saginaw
- Muskegon
- Grand Rapids
- Port Huron
- Flint
- Holland
- Lansing
- Jackson
- Detroit
- Kalamazoo
- Ann Arbor
- Lake Erie

Lake Superior

CANADA

Lake Michigan

0   70 mi.

N W E S

CANADA

| Central Lower Peninsula | Indiana | Ohio |

East Lansing is the home of Michigan State University (MSU). This university was founded in 1855 as Michigan **Agricultural** College. It was the first agricultural college in the United States. The school originally promoted modern methods of growing crops and raising **livestock.** For the first time, students could take farming-related classes for college credit. Today, MSU offers courses in every subject and field of study.

Jackson was a center for coal mining in the 1800s. Coal production here lasted only a short while because the coal was not the best quality for fuel.

LAND AND WATER

The central Lower Peninsula is generally flat with a few gently rolling hills. The region has many **rural** areas with farms and small towns. The central Lower Peninsula has rivers, streams, and lakes as well.

"Sparty" is the mascot of the Michigan State University Spartans.

Creating Counties

It took surveyors from 1815 until 1851 to measure all of the land in Michigan. Land surveys helped people to know the exact boundaries of their land. Michigan is divided into squares. Each 1-mile by 1-mile square is called a section. Thirty-six sections make a township that is 6 miles by 6 miles. Most counties have 16 to 20 townships. Roads follow along the township lines. Astronauts in low orbit around the Earth can actually see the square shape of Michigan's townships as light-colored lines.

There are more than 600 natural lakes around the city of Jackson alone. The Grand River, the longest river in the state, is in this region. The river runs for about 260 miles. Its **origin** is south of the city of Jackson. The Grand River flows north and then begins to travel westward in Lansing until it empties into Lake Michigan at Spring Lake.

CLIMATE

Because of its distance from all of the Great Lakes, this area is not affected by the **lake effect** factor. The average high temperature in Lansing in July is 83°F. The average low temperature in January is 14°F. The average annual rainfall is 32 inches and the average snowfall each year is 55 inches.

GOVERNMENT SERVICE INDUSTRY

Government service is one of the major **occupations** in this region. There are thousands of state employees working in government agencies and in the public school system throughout the state.

AUTOMOBILE INDUSTRY

The central Lower Peninsula has also played a big part in the start of the automobile **industry** in Michigan. In the early 1900s, this was where Ransom Olds created a practical motor vehicle. He wanted to build a vehicle that cost about the same as a horse and buggy. The first automobile factory in the United States opened in Lansing. Ransom Olds built the world's first mass-produced automobile, the 1901 Oldsmobile Curved Dash Runabout. The city of Lansing would become a leader in the automobile industry and has been the headquarters of General Motor's Oldsmobile division. The Oldsmobile division will be closing after the 2004 models are completed.

Ransom Olds

Chemical Industry

When the logging was finished in the area near Midland, that city became important for another reason. In 1890, a chemist named Herbert H. Dow did experiments to **extract** chemicals from the **salt brine** that is deep in the ground in this region. As a result of his work, Dow Chemical Company was formed. To this day, the company continues to produce many products that are used every day. In their factories they make personal care products, **pharmaceuticals,** and plastics.

Agriculture Industry

Crop farming and dairy farming are important in this region. Milk and milk products from the central Lower Peninsula are sold to larger Michigan cities like Detroit, Grand Rapids, and Flint. **Livestock,** including hogs, sheep, and poultry, are raised and sold in this region.

There are more than 4,000 dairy farms in Michigan.

The Michigan Space and Science Center has a piece of moon rock collected by Jackson astronaut Al Worden's Apollo-15 team.

Some farms grow hay, corn, and oats to feed the **livestock.** Other farms raise wheat, corn, and soybeans as **cash crops.** Also grown in the central Lower Peninsula are tomatoes, sweet corn, squash, melons, cabbage, and potatoes.

TOURIST ATTRACTIONS AND PLACES OF INTEREST

Visitors can climb into a real space capsule at Michigan Space and Science Center in Jackson. Also on display are moon rocks, the Apollo 9 command module, space suits, and an 85-foot rocket.

There are tours of the **capitol** building in Lansing. When this white sandstone building replaced a brick one in 1789, it was the first capitol building in the country to imitate the style of the U.S. Capitol in Washington, D.C. Michigan's capitol has a large white dome and wings of offices on both sides of the center. There are 19 chandeliers in the Capitol made from copper and iron mined in the Upper Peninsula. Each lamp weighs about 400 pounds and was designed by Tiffany & Company in New York.

Michigan Historical Museum, in the Capitol Complex, has an interesting exhibit of the story of Michigan's settlement and **industry.** The building surrounds a three-story tall, living white pine tree. Museum visitors pass through a small, recreated copper mine and lumber camp.

Just a short walk from the capitol is the Impression 5 Museum. Using all five senses, visitors can try more than 200 experiments. This is one of the best hands-on science museums in the United States, and it was especially designed for students in grades 4 through 6.

Western Lower Peninsula

The western Lower Peninsula is the sunset side of the state. Some people call it Michigan's West Coast. Along the Lake Michigan shoreline, there are miles of sandy beaches and tall sand dunes. To the south there is the famous fruit belt of Michigan. **Inland** there is the busy city of Grand Rapids, the largest city in the western Lower Peninsula.

Michigan's Western Lower Peninsula

Grand Rapids is named for the rapids on the Grand River that runs through the downtown area.

LOCATION AND MAJOR CITIES

Grand Rapids is the second largest city in Michigan, following only Detroit. It has a population of about 197,800. Grand Rapids is part of a **metropolitan** area, similar to metropolitan Detroit. The metropolitan area is called the West Michigan Metro Tri-Plex and includes more than 100 cities, townships, and villages. The major cities in this metropolitan area are Grand Rapids, Muskegon, and Holland. About 1.1 million people live in the West Michigan Metro Tri-Plex.

The western Lower Peninsula is known for its production of office furniture, automotive supplies, and fruit farming.

Dutch **immigrants** settled the city called Holland. They brought their farming skills to this state. Growing celery was their specialty. Today, Michigan still ranks second in the United States in the harvest of this vegetable.

"Cereal Bowl of America"

In the late 1800s, Dr. John Kellogg ran the Battle Creek Sanitarium, which was something like a health spa. He encouraged people to eat good foods and live a healthier life. One thing he invented was the first dry breakfast cereal. He believed that cereal was better for you than sausage, eggs, and hash browns. Today Battle Creek produces more breakfast cereal than any other city in the world.

Muskegon was a big lumber town on Lake Michigan in the 1800s. At one time there were 47 sawmills. This city is now a mixture of **manufacturing** and **tourism.**

Lake Michigan beaches are popular with boaters, swimmers, outdoor sports lovers, and sunset watchers.

LAND AND WATER

The western Lower Peninsula is quite flat with some rolling hills and fields. Sand dune formations rise along the Lake Michigan shoreline. There are many **inland** lakes, rivers, and streams. The Grand River is the largest river in the region.

CLIMATE

The western Lower Peninsula is the region most affected by the **lake effect** factor. After the sunshine of summer, the water of Lake Michigan will stay warm for a long time. Cool fall breezes blow across the lake, but they are warmed before they reach land. This makes the **climate** and soil good for growing fruit. The fruit has longer to ripen and there is more time for new tree growth to be stronger before winter. After winter, the water in Lake Michigan is cooler than the warm spring breezes. As winds blow across the lake now, they are cooled down. This prevents fruit buds from blossoming too soon. The lake effect factor helps the blossoms stay closed until the danger of frost has passed. This creates a long growing season that lasts up to 170 days.

The average temperatures are similar along the lakeshore and inland. It often feels cooler by the water though, because of breezes over the wide open space of the lake. In Grand Rapids, the average high temperature in July is 83°F and the average low temperature in January is 15°F. The average annual rainfall is 38 inches. Snowfall

Robinette's Apple Haus and Gift Barn in Grand Rapids is a popular place to pick fruit and take hayrides.

is higher closest to Lake Michigan. The average annual snowfall in Holland is 89.9 inches and in Grand Rapids is 71.6 inches. The highest recorded temperature in Grand Rapids was 100°F in 1988 and the lowest temperature was −21°F in 1979.

AGRICULTURE INDUSTRY

Native Americans were the first to recognize the value of the rich soil in this region. They grew corn, beans, peas, squash, and pumpkins. The settlers cleared land for their homes and began to farm the land. They discovered that the western Lower Peninsula was good for farming. Fruit trees **thrive** here. Michigan became one of the leading producers of apples, blueberries, cantaloupes, cherries, grapes, peaches, pears, plums, raspberries, and strawberries. Because bees are attracted to fruit blossoms, honey is another product from this region. Many vegetables also grow well here, especially asparagus, bell peppers, carrots, cauliflower, celery, cucumbers, onions, potatoes, pumpkins, snap beans, sweet corn, and tomatoes.

Steelcase, Inc. has been part of the Grand Rapids community since 1912.

FURNITURE INDUSTRY

As the Grand River flows toward Lake Michigan, it passes through many big and little towns. One city where the river had a major impact is the city of Grand Rapids. This city was only a trading post in 1826 but really began to grow when the logging **industry** was strong. Lumber from hardwood trees was plentiful in the region. Grand Rapids was located right on the river, which provided water power and

Children holding decorated windmill blades march in the Kinderparade every year during Holland's Tulip Time Festival.

transportation. Furniture makers settled in the area. At first, individuals or small partnerships made the furniture, and it was sold in the community. The first furniture factories started in Grand Rapids in the mid-1800s. By 1900, there were about 85 furniture companies here. They were able to ship their product by boats and trains to other states. Grand Rapids earned a reputation for quality furniture and became known as the "Furniture Capital of the World." Today, the furniture made in the Grand Rapids area is mostly office furniture. Steelcase, Inc. is the largest office furniture **manufacturer** in the world. Two other important office furniture companies in the region are Herman Miller and Haworth. A major portion of the office furniture used around the world is manufactured here.

TOURIST ATTRACTIONS AND PLACES OF INTEREST

The Kalamazoo Air Zoo has a collection of aircraft, including planes that flew during World War II, the Korean War, the Vietnam War, and the Persian Gulf war. These are planes called Flying Tigers, Gooney Bird, Tin Goose, Aircobra, and Grumman Cats. That is why this is called a zoo.

More than 4.4 million tulip bulbs blossom each spring for the Tulip Time Festival in the city of Holland. Many of the people of Holland wear traditional Dutch costumes and wooden shoes that day and participate in a street washing parade.

This horse is one of the most popular sculptures at Meijer Gardens. It is one of the biggest horse sculptures in the world.

Shivering Timbers is one of the many roller coaster rides at Michigan's Adventure and Wild Water Amusement Park in Muskegon. The park also features almost 50 rides and water slides.

Frederik Meijer Gardens and Sculpture Park is 125 acres of indoor and outdoor gardens and trails. There are many sculptures along the trails. The most amazing sculpture is a huge, 24-foot tall bronze horse designed by Leonardo da Vinci.

You can take a charter fishing boat ride from Grand Haven and catch perch, coho and chinook salmon, steelhead, whitefish, and lake and brown trout in Lake Michigan.

The curved roof of the $220 million DeVos Place convention center in downtown Grand Rapids is designed to imitate the flow of the Grand River outside its windows. The convention center is immense. The main exhibit hall is the size of three football fields side by side. There are no columns in the middle. The building is high enough to hold a Ferris wheel inside.

Any eighteen-wheel truck that can drive on Michigan highways can drive right through the delivery doors and into the De Vos Place exhibit hall.

Map of Michigan

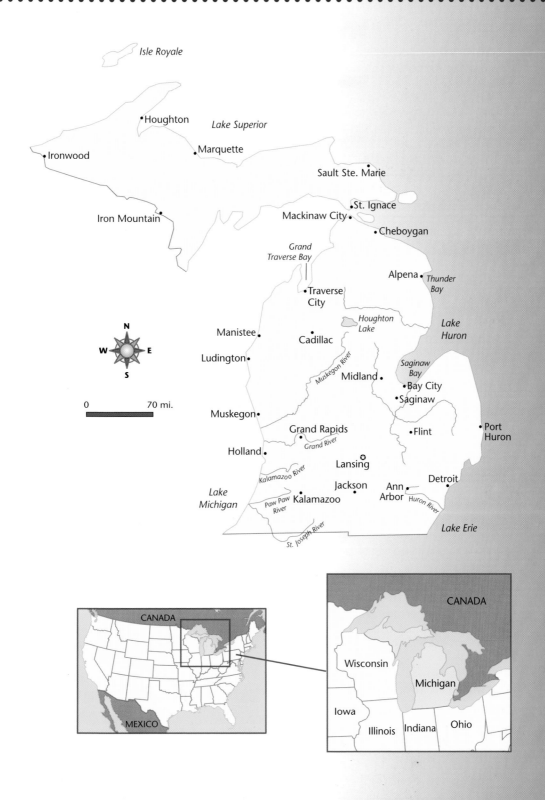

Glossary

agriculture farming

ammunition objects fired from guns or explosives used in war

arsenal place where military equipment is made and stored

artifact something created by humans for a practical purpose during a certain time period

assassinate murder an important person by surprise attack

authentic based on real life

axle shaft on which a wheel turns

barren unable to grow plants

capital location of a government

capitol building in which the legislature meets

cargo goods carried by ship, plane, or vehicle

cash crop something grown to sell for profit

citizen person who lives in a city, town, state, or country

civil rights rights of personal liberty guaranteed by the U.S. Constitution

climate weather conditions that are usual for a certain area

commerce buying and selling goods

conservation planned management of natural resources to prevent waste, destruction, or neglect

densely crowded together

economy control of money that is earned and spent in a home, business, or government

era important period in history

export good or service sent out of the country for profit

extract to get out by pressing, distilling, or by a chemical process

fertile bearing crops or vegetation in abundance

fort strong building used for defense against enemy attack

geologist scientist who studies earth science

immigrant one who moves to another country to settle

import bring a good or service into the country

industry group of businesses that offer a similar product or service

inland not near the coast

innovation new idea, method, or device

lake effect snow caused by cool winds picking up moisture as they blow over warm water

livestock farm animals raised for profit

manufacture make goods by hand or machine

mastodon prehistoric relative of today's elephant

metropolitan area surrounding a large city

natural resource something from nature that is available to take care of a need

occupation career or job

ore rock or mineral from which a metal can be obtained

origin beginning

overcutting taking down too many trees without replacing them by planting new ones

peninsula piece of land that is surrounded by water on three sides

pharmaceutical type of medication

port place where ships load and unload cargo

pulp material prepared from wood that is used to make paper

reenactment repeat something that has happened before

reforestation to renew forest growth by planting new trees

remote far off in place and time

resort place where people go for pleasure

rural having to do with the country or farmland

salt brine water containing a lot of salt

semi-maritime type of climate that is affected by nearby water

sparsely not thickly settled

suburb city or town just outside a larger city

tannin substance often made from oak bark or hemlock and used for dyeing, tanning, and making ink

territory area with its own government that is not part of a state

thrive do very well

tourism industry built around people who travel for pleasure

vintage time when something was made

wetland very wet, low-lying area

More Books to Read

Lytle, Robert A. *Mackinac Passage: Mystery at Round Island Light.* Auburn Hill, Mich.: Edco Publishing, 2001.

McConnell, David B. *Our Michigan Adventure.* Hillsdale, Mich.: Hillsdale Educational Publishers, 2002.

Panagopoulos, Janie Lynn. *Madame Cadillac's Ghost: A Great Lakes Adventure in History and Mystery.* Spring Lake, Mich.: River Road Publications, 2002.

Panagopoulos, Janie Lynn. *The Runes of Isle Royale: A Great Lakes Adventure in History and Mystery.* Spring Lake, Mich.: River Road, 2000.

Peckham, Linda R. and Lori Ellen Heuft. *Saw Mills and Sleigh Bells: Stories of Mid-Michigan Settlers.* Williamston, Mich.: Catalpa Publications, 1999.

Tuitel, Johnnie. *Discovery on Blackbird Island.* Norton Shores, Mich.: Cedar Tree Publications, 2000.

Whelan, Gloria. *The Wanigan: A Life on the River.* New York: Knopf, 2002.

Index

About the Author

Alexandra Fix is the mother of five grown readers, a son and four daughters. She and her husband are both Michigan natives. Creating a home has been her first love, but close behind is her love of books. Her earliest career was as a registered nurse, but since 1990, she has been an elementary school librarian in Grand Rapids. While her kids were growing up, she completed a BA with a major in English. Her freelance writing currently includes book reviews and feature articles for a West Michigan magazine.